T0365022

Home

Finding Your Place in the Family of God

JENNIFER CARAVANTES

WESTBOW
P R E S S®
A DIVISION OF THOMAS NELSON
& ZONDERVAN

Scripture quotations marked MSG are taken from THE MESSAGE.
Copyright 1993, 1994, 1995, 1996, 2000, 2001, 2002, 2003 by Eugene
H. Peterson. Used by permission of NavPress Publishing Group.

Scripture quotations marked NKJV are taken from the New King James Version.
Copyright 1982 by Thomas Nelson, Inc. Used by permission. All rights reserved.

GOD'S WORD® translation. Copyrighted © 1995 by God's Word to the Nations.
Text is currently under stewardship of Baker Publishing Group, Ada, MI.

Scripture quotations marked KJV are from the Holy Bible, King James
Version (Authorized Version). First published in 1611. Quoted from the KJV
Classic Reference Bible, Copyright 1983 by The Zondervan Corporation.

WestBow Press books may be ordered through booksellers or by contacting:

WestBow Press
A Division of Thomas Nelson & Zondervan
1663 Liberty Drive
Bloomington, IN 47403
www.westbowpress.com
1 (866) 928-1240

Because of the dynamic nature of the Internet, any web addresses or
links contained in this book may have changed since publication and
may no longer be valid. The views expressed in this work are solely those
of the author and do not necessarily reflect the views of the publisher,
and the publisher hereby disclaims any responsibility for them.

Any people depicted in stock imagery provided by Thinkstock are models,
and such images are being used for illustrative purposes only.
Certain stock imagery © Thinkstock.

ISBN: 978-1-5127-7692-8 (sc)
ISBN: 978-1-5127-7693-5 (e)

Library of Congress Control Number: 2017902975

Print information available on the last page.

WestBow Press rev. date: 03/16/2017

DEDICATION

This book is dedicated to my husband, my parents, my siblings, and my mentor, Mama C.

I love you all. Derek, you are the most incredible man. You never cease to amaze me with how you respond to life. You inspire me daily. Your wisdom and steadfast love have made me the happiest bride. Thank you for supporting me in this. I love you. To my parents, for never giving up when the road home was marked with many mistakes on my part and for your unconditional love. To my siblings for making me laugh, your endless support, and being who you are. You are wonderful, and I love you dearly. To my Mama C for the almost weekly phone calls for years as you processed life with me. You taught me more than I can write in this small space. Thank you to the extended church family who fanned the flame in me. I love you! And special thanks to my Savior, Jesus. You have made the journey home worth every step! I love you, and I'm forever grateful to be home.

Long before he laid down earth's foundations, he had us in mind, had settled on us as the focus of his love, to be made whole and holy by his love. Long, long ago he decided to adopt us into his family through Jesus Christ. (What pleasure he took in planning this!) He wanted us to enter into the celebration of his lavish gift-giving by the hand of his beloved Son. (Ephesians 1:4–6 MSG)

Contents

INTRODUCTION

Hi. I'm glad you're here. If you are looking to find horror stories of my growing up as a pastor's kid during the '80s and '90s, you won't find that here. If you are looking to find an enchanted book with nothing but pure bliss, I encourage you to stop reading now. This book isn't meant to make you feel sensational emotions or to stir up dramatic memories.

Rather, I write because there is something about family that is incredibly dear to God's heart. And whether we were born into great families or not, somehow and in some fashion, we all can relate to that word.

Over the past thirty years, I have seen people come and go in their church attendance while others have altogether quit going. I struggle with that. I wonder what is it about people's experiences of God or the family of God that brought them to the place of deciding to leave home.

Just like we can't choose the family we are born into, we don't get to choose the people God brings into the family either. Whatever the reason is for why you are reading this book, I pray it blesses you. I pray that it gives you a better understanding of just how incredibly valuable you are to the family of God and how much you matter. And in this moment, I want to say I'm sorry. I'm sorry for the pain, the hurt, or maybe the betrayal you felt at one point or another in your life from the family of God. I'm sorry for the intentional or unintentional moments that left your faith reeling with uncertainty. And I'm sorry for the times when it was maybe people in the church that hurt you the most and made you never want to go back to church. I ask that you reconsider your place in

xii

the family of God. Sure, maybe you need to go to a different church if it was super unhealthy and for legitimate reasons, but if you have lost heart, I pray you find the courage to take the journey home. You are not unwanted. Whether you've been away for two weeks, two months, or twenty years, it's not too late. It's never too late. Your Father loves you. "That is why you are no longer foreigners and outsiders but citizens together with God's people and members of God's family" (Ephesians 2:19 GW). Thank you for sharing this journey with me. Shall we begin?

CHAPTER 1

PASTORS' KIDS: ARE THEY REALLY THAT WILD?

Is it really true about us—you know, that we are fettered and just waiting to go ballistic in sinful vices once left to our own selves? I don't know. Read on, and you tell me.

I grew up in a non-denominational church during the '80s, and I feel like my siblings and I were fairly sheltered. The biggest topic I remember in my little life was when the rapture was going to take place. Mostly I wondered what would happen if I was left behind. I grew up listening to "Focus on the Family" on the radio, reading *Brio* magazine, and listening to "DC Talk" and worship music. We didn't watch anything past PG until we were in our teen years. We lived a conservative life, especially being from a rural town where cable television was spotty.

My dad was saved during the Jesus Movement in the '70s, and there was a beautiful emphasis on holiness. He was radically saved and never looked back. My mom was a Jesus lover from practically birth, and for her, following Jesus came naturally. She was a pastor's kid and got married right out of high school. Having a glass of wine to relax was never a priority for her. She would tell us she didn't need to open a door to find out later it was a snare. She let Jesus be her comforter and instead chose to speak scripture at the storms in her life. That has never failed her.

Growing up, church was always just sort of there. However, I knew we were being taught the way, and I knew it was right. It was our routine to go to church every Sunday, and we did mostly except for when we were sick or on vacation. The church was just down the street from our house, so I would often go and pray. I would pray for whatever came to mind.

I also loved it when we would have evangelists and special speakers come to town, because it meant staying up late after meetings. In addition, there was something different in the air at the meetings—perhaps anticipation. I remember one of my favorite songs the worship team played in church growing up was, "We Are Standing on Holy Ground." I still love that song to this day. Reflecting back, I remember times where the anointing was so tangible that even as a child, I knew Jesus was there in a special way. The room felt different, and I never wanted the service to end.

Those moments were some of the most tangible moments of God being real in my young life. There were healings, salvations, deliverances, and people responding to the love of God. Those moments revealed something much bigger than just myself or anyone else in the room. I saw a glimpse of a God who is bigger than any dysfunction, bigger than any pain, bigger than any disease. Nothing was off limits to His mercy and love. I cherish those memories dearly.

Aside from church, I remember seeing my parents leave countless times to do counseling sessions. I watched as they gave away resources they couldn't replace. I watched as they took children into our home who needed a place to stay. There have been countless hospital visits over the tenure of their twenty-seven-plus years in ministry. I remember numerous times they opened our home to feed people. Our home was a continuous place where people wanted to be. They weren't just pastors to people; they became like parents to some. I saw my mom consistently believe the best about someone even if he or she had broken her heart. She chose not to ever become jaded. I saw them do outreaches, events, and Sunday after Sunday show up for years. They didn't stop loving people. They haven't stopped either. They have given their lives for the sake of the cross, to make Jesus known. They have given their time, their resources, their hearts, their all. I have yet to meet two people as generous as them. Generosity flows out of supernatural love. They have it, and it's incredible.

We were not the perfect family. There were struggles as my parents raised three kids almost at poverty level in their early years while pastoring a small church and being incredibly young themselves. They had a lot on their plates.

I can say that many of the issues I went through as a child were from me *feeling* all the time. I didn't like that. I didn't want to feel. Feelings became my truth, and this erupted into an eating disorder by the eighth grade as I transitioned from a private Christian school into a public one. I didn't want to feel fat. I didn't want to feel rejected … I didn't want to feel like an outsider as a Christian. I went on to outgrow that by the end of my eighth-grade year but had relapses for the next fifteen years. High school flew by with not being *pretty enough* for the guys to date. I was their buddy. I struggled with finding connection and acceptance. I had one boyfriend in the four years of high school. During those years, I felt an immense tug of war in my life as I bounced between church on Sundays and the six days between that. The desire to be accepted weighed on me continuously, and I started praying less, reading my Bible less, and distancing myself from God and the church.

I did not want much to do with God if all I was going to get was mocked for being a Christian. I believed God was trying to take away all the fun. I wanted to be able to do things without feeling like I was sinning all the time. I didn't want to just obey Him and His rules and not get—what I felt—was anything in return. To be honest, I was tired of trying.

I became offended at God. The battle for my faith was on. It started with unmet expectations that I had of Him. His character didn't seem to match my ideology. Therefore, my theology was becoming challenged by this. I began questioning His goodness and wondering if His word was nothing more than empty promises. The following five statements swirled in my mind.

If God is _____.

Why would He _____.

How could He let _____.

Where was He when _____.

When I needed Him the most He _____.

These statements are then mixed with five emotions:

- fear

- anger

- disappointment

- hopelessness

- indifference

I was heartbroken before I was even eighteen. In my childlike mind, I couldn't understand why God wasn't who I thought He was. I didn't understand why people had to go through certain things. I couldn't figure out why prayers were going unanswered for so long. All those moments I spent at the church praying seemed to flood my mind, and the reality was most of those prayers weren't answered. The pain of that swirled in my heart. I didn't understand why marriages weren't healed. I didn't understand sickness. I couldn't marry the reality of my perceptions with the stories I was reading in my Bible. I felt abandoned. I felt confused. I wanted Him to be real in my life and not just something or someone I read about in the Bible.

I graduated high school and moved away to go to college. I would try to connect at churches and I remember the immense feeling of being "too secular" for the church, but too "churchy" for the world. It was like living in this incredibly weird limbo. I had to choose.

I chose the ones that were reaching out to me the most. It wasn't the church. So, I followed.

CHAPTER 2

∽

FOR HE SO LOVED.

I fashioned you. Little you.

I picked out your hair.

Long or short?

Do I add curls and waves or leave it straight?

I formed your little face.

I picked your eyes.

Eyes that would see My glory.

Blue, brown, or hazel?

I picked the ones perfect for you.

For God so loved ...

I chose your hands, your feet, then added your nails.

Long legs or short?
I chose the ones for My perfect little you.
I loved you from before you were born.
I saw you.
You have always been on my mind.

My perfect little you, I wanted the world to know you.
I picked the time and date for you to be born.
Don't despise me for this.
I knew you would face things.
Great things, many things.

This is precisely why I promised to never leave My perfect little you.
How can you think for one moment I am unjust?
Do I take pleasure in your pain?
No! Never!
You are My perfect little one.

Choices, sin, mistakes won't stop Me! They won't stop Me!
They will not stop My love for you.
I have sent My Son for you,

For My perfect little one.

I long for you so much.

I will not let anything come between us.

Not heights. Not depths. Nothing.

Nothing can stop my love toward you.

You are forever My perfect little you.

CHAPTER 3

TAKING YOUR KIDS TO WORK

It's Monday morning, and as you make your way to the kitchen, you look at your wife with bewilderment and notice your three kids are still home. They should've left for school ten minutes ago. Your wife reminds you about the e-mail from your boss last week. He has decided every Monday your children will be shadowing you at work for two hours as part of what he described as a work study enrichment program for the future generation. Your mind goes foggy as you try to recall exactly what it was he called it.

You silently wonder if your boss has decided to slowly start phasing you out of your job or if he just sincerely doesn't like you. Either way, your thoughts are interrupted by two arguing children in your car and the other one honking at you. You tell your wife good-bye as she tries to assure you it won't be that bad. Your mind swirls as you think of your colossal project you are pitching that day to not only your boss and colleagues but prospective clients as well. On your commute, you brief them on the project and bribe them to sit quietly through the presentation by offering to take them mini golfing and to a movie that weekend.

You arrive to work and start the presentation moments later. You hit every point you had meticulously planned. You ask if there are any questions and listen silently. You can't tell if the silence is because they are secretly envying your brilliant strategies or if they are wondering how you ever managed to get hired in the first place. Either way, there isn't any discussion. The meeting is over. As you are packing up your items, you think to yourself how seemingly easy that was.

Before you are done, one of your colleagues comes over to give you some … "constructive" feedback … in front of your kids. They listen as their dad's work is suddenly not so well received. They notice how well you take it but soon see another coworker come up and say something as well. This time it's a little more hushed, but it doesn't matter. The kids see that exchange too. What they see was their dad's work isn't as grand in others' eyes as it is in their own. The short-lived approval they basked in was soon shattered by the two naysayers. Week after week they watch the various interactions their dad has at work—his conversations, his phone calls, the deadlines, the meetings—and their world becomes colored by the crowd their father has to please.

For most men, who find such pride and fulfillment in their work, I'm not exactly sure it would be a welcoming invitation to have their children weekly job shadow. For a pastor's kids that's exactly what we do. We watch. We listen. We take it all in. Week after week. We aren't privy to certain meetings. And my parents didn't discuss confidential things with us. I'm not talking about that at all. We didn't have to be necessarily told anything. It's the undertones in the room that can create the greatest noise. And on Sundays, it's the lack thereof that tends to scream the loudest. As a pastor's kid, our world is shaped by the interactions that take place in and outside of the church. We are keenly aware of the upsets and the wins.

I can't imagine the pressure pastors face to be dad and pastor. And I wonder if they fear letting their children down both publicly and privately. Friend, when was the last time you took your child to work with you? When was the last time your child listened as you gave a presentation to your boss and listened to the feedback given to you? My parents' church is amazing. I'm not saying this is something that happened all the time or even remotely most of the time. And it's not that you can't have those discussions with your pastor or that you shouldn't. It's simply remembering that no pastor is perfect. No pastor is going to always say everything you agree with. No pastor is ever going to fit the perfect mold. However, I think that we fail to understand sometimes the immense pressure we place on our pastors. We forget about their families, and about their children and maybe what they notice, and that we all are part of a bigger family, and there is no such thing as a perfect one. I don't know, but as a pastor's kid, I kind of get attached to the people I do life with. I consider you family. You are family. Beloved, we need to grasp the reality of what it does when we leave the church without an explanation, church hop, or just show up once a month. It's painful and costly. It's like a family split.

It's also knowing that if you leave because of some unmet expectation you have, then it's probably not the right reason to leave. And you will be missed, because chances are you still belong to that family. You might think the "whole" family of God is where you belong, but you probably aren't going to build strong relationships with millions of people. Strength and community happen on a much smaller scale. And while you may think you aren't missed, you are.

There is something unique about you that belongs to that church family for that season. Our culture has been described as the "throwaway" culture. We are so used to everything being replaceable that we easily discard. That can be said for relationships too with our church family. Are we willing to stick around? It takes work, but it's so incredibly worth it!

And to you, dear reader, if you were a pastor, worship leader, or in some sort of vocational ministry and walked away because of wounds and the pressure being too intense, I ask that you find your way back. Maybe you were let go, fired, demoted, or overlooked. I'm not sure. Or maybe it was a church split or you were replaced by a younger individual with far less experience and passion. Don't despair. Your kingdom assignment didn't start with man's approval, nor does it end when none is given. Whatever pain has pushed your purpose to the sidelines for the past few years or even many years, for that matter, doesn't determine where you're going. A detour is never a dead end with your Father. I pray the wounds caused by the church family are eternally healed in you and your family in this moment by the unconquerable love of your God! Maybe you resigned because of some sort of sin or failure. That too can be covered in the redeeming blood of Jesus. His plans are far bigger. It was said that after David killed Goliath they asked who his father was (see I Samuel 17:55). Your greatest victory just might still be ahead of you... and your Father is right there cheering you on. He doesn't raise powerless sons and daughters. He raised you to defeat giants.

Your kingdom assignment didn't start with man's approval, nor does it end when none is given.

Chapter 4

FINDING YOUR MISSION FIELD

I remember sometime in 2012 asking the Lord and praying for months about what my life would look like in the new place my husband and I were living. I was lonely. My husband would go to work each day, and there I was by myself trying to fill up my day. I would go jogging and pray about what I was to do there. I didn't know hardly anyone, and I wanted connection and belonging. I knew there were other women in my community like me. Maybe they weren't lonely, but I knew they were looking for connection.

Eventually I met two sweet gals who didn't want to go to church, and I wondered how I could be a blessing to them right where they were. I wanted to make myself available to them now. Because I was bored, I was struggling with having myself on my mind all the time, and I knew the best thing to do was to get *me* off my mind and begin serving at my church. I had done this previously in another city we lived in and knew how important it was to get plugged in at my local church. I began to volunteer there and eventually came on staff. I remember Pastor Shawn always quoting, "The Word became flesh and blood and moved into the neighborhood" (John 1:14 MSG). That stuck with me.

I spoke with some of my friends over coffee at my neighborhood Starbucks about reaching out the two gals I had met. We also knew there were other women in the community who weren't going to church or even wanting to go. We discussed the possibilities, and I went back to my cubicle at work and asked one of my coworkers if she wanted to go to the park with me the following Thursday. We would call it "Thursday Happenings." She said yes. We would essentially be a small group in a park, building community and connection on a lawn. Sounds like an unlikely place, but that's exactly where I felt we were to go.

So, there we were—my coworker and me, our very own small group with the covering and blessing of our pastor and church. I cannot tell you what a difference that makes! I must digress on this for just a moment. If you are trying to go do ministry or a work for God without being under some form of leadership, I can almost guarantee a disaster. Sure, it may be nice for a few weeks, months, or years, but you and the passion will wear out, and the lack of oversight doesn't do anyone any good. It's terribly naïve to think otherwise.

If you are tempted to leave a church and start a small group as a substitute for church, I again encourage you to at least find another church or leadership to be your covering. And no, your

Jennifer Caravantes

husband isn't the only covering. You both need it if you are going to be leading a home church or group. Isolated or likeminded people will often huddle where there is no authentic leadership. It becomes more about the cause than Jesus himself.

> **Isolated or likeminded people will often huddle where there is no authentic leadership.**

Okay, back to the story. We brought some snacks and some beverages and were hoping to be a blessing. Week after week I would go up to lovely ladies I spotted in the park and introduce myself. Trust me, it wasn't necessarily easy. I don't particularly enjoy ambushing people asking them to join my group. I mean, it did sound a little junior highish.

On top of that, I can't tell you what it felt like walking up to women who looked perfect with their yoga pants and aviator sunglasses, holding a Starbucks skinny latte. And there I was a hot mess, literally. My hair was half frizzed out from the summer heat, and I felt the sweat start to bead as I nervously tried to think of a way to make myself sound confident. I often tried to start a conversation with something about fashion or some easy topic that helped ease the nerves. The thing is, it's not about our comfort; it's about our mission. And you know what? I'm so thankful it wasn't about staying in my comfort zone. Some of the gals would join us, and others didn't. Slowly our group grew. Months of weekly meetings evolved into a beautiful group of women who shared life together. The church would host parties, have prizes for the moms, and provide a platform for gathering. Through that group, I came to know some of the most beautiful and kind-hearted women.

> ### *It's not about our comfort;*
> ### *it's about our mission.*

The goal of the group wasn't to preach at them. In fact, we didn't invite them to church after they had been coming for a bit. They weren't there to be baited, then converted. That's not family. The two women who I originally had in mind when I started the group never came. Others did, though. Several others. In fact, I was told about ten of those families ended up getting plugged in at the church.

You see, ultimately my goal was for them to know how much the Father loves them, but I am not an evangelist. I don't enjoy asking people on the spot if they want to get saved. I wish I was bolder. Hear me when I say this: *if I would have thought about what I am not, I would have never done anything.* In addition to that, had I been so set on the two gals coming and making a big fuss over that, I would have completely missed out on the handiwork He was doing before my eyes. What Thursday Happenings taught me was that there is community all around me if I am willing to take the time for it. There are others who are looking for it too and are simply waiting for the invitation. It's incredibly easy to hide behind our busyness and fears because hiding always makes sense. I kid. It never does.

> **Every place you ever find yourself**
> **you have a ministry there.**

Friend, what is your mission field? What is the thing you have felt God place on your heart for years, and you have yet to leave the shores to walk on the waves? Where is your mission field? Is it your workplace? Is it starting a small group at your college campus? Is it volunteering at your local food bank? What are you waiting for? It says in 2 Timothy 3:17 (GW) that you are "Completely prepared to do good things." He's equipped you by giving you what you need to do good things. Do you know how many people are lonely? Do you know how many people can be surrounded by people but inside are dying because they feel so alone?

So what if you tried before and things didn't turn out as you thought? So what if you think you are too old or too young or too whatever, for that matter? You are enough. You're not alone either. Jesus is with you every step of the way. If you are thinking you have tried something before and it failed, don't despair! You don't quit looking for love because you go on one bad date. Just because you may have had a misstep once or even several times, it doesn't mean you give up altogether! You are priceless, and you have something to offer! Talk to your pastor or talk to your leadership, and allow them to help you find ways you can be a part of the family with your unique talents. Because every place you ever find yourself, you have a ministry there, whether it's to one or ten thousand. Only God knows, but He's waiting for you.

The Word became flesh and blood and moved into the neighborhood. (John 1:14 MSG)

CHAPTER 5

THE JOURNEY HOME

He hath made us accepted in the
Beloved. (Ephesians 1:6 KJV)

Journal Entry

Last week I felt this terrible struggle—a feeling
that is hard to describe. It was something I
couldn't understand. In the midst of all the pain
and fear I've gone through, I've struggled. What
if I don't believe He is big? Maybe it's my wanting
to understand? Maybe logic is in collision with
my spirit. Perhaps my logic is wanting to override
by all means necessary to get the answer it wants.

After all, I deserve to know. I have settled for nothing less than explanations from a God who refuses to be controlled.

> *I have settled for nothing less*
> *than explanations from a God*
> *who refuses to be controlled.*

Maybe my words are not finding the heart of my feelings. My feelings have been hurt by You for not doing what I think you can easily do in Your great power. Because maybe when I read Your word I hear the words from a man who endured far more than I, I am hit with this

> "And blessed is he who is not offended because of Me" (Matthew 11:6 NKJV)

Maybe I hide behind my prayers and Bible reading well. I know You are my answer, yet hate that the answer has not been fully manifested in my life. Then I wonder if it is You or if it's me. Which one of us is not living up to my expectation? My expectations of You come from my sinfulness—from pride. I'm having a hard time letting you be God in my life. The short stints of trying hard have only created a track record of defeat. And I'm left with anger at not being "there" when I've been "here" for a so long. So I'm back to self-preservation, pride, and self-pity. I've been unknowingly trying to figure You out. Consequently, my faith has become smaller, and so have You, because I demanded a God I can understand in order that I may not be offended at Him.

I demanded a God I can understand in order that I may not be offended at Him.

By doing this, it keeps the margins safe and within the boundaries of reason. And if You or I ever deviate, it's back to me trying to control. I want to control the outcomes. But in truth, what I am really looking for is to live a life that is not controlling or controlled but in the simplicity of relationship.

***

During the early 2000s in my college years, I continued in a series of self-destructive choices, causing much pain to myself and those around me. I lived my life out of rejection and never wanted to be completely vulnerable, so I drank and partied. The problem with not allowing myself to be accepted into the Beloved was that I wanted others to not only accept me but find my sinful lifestyle acceptable. It no longer was about freedom and love. I erroneously thought that if people around me found my behavior acceptable then I was accepted.

It was a false sense of belonging, much like today's culture. It's not about freedom. When you realize how much you are accepted, there is outflow from that. You aren't looking for acceptance outside of the Trinity (Father, Son, and Holy Spirit). All other relationships are a byproduct of the fullness of being accepted into the Beloved. It doesn't matter if someone doesn't agree with you on this or that. You no longer need the acceptance because you've already been accepted. No longer do you need to convince people to hear your voice and accept it, because you know the One who is altogether lovely hears your voice and that's what matters. This all comes from the fullness of knowing how incredibly dear you are to your Father.

I erroneously thought that if people around me found my behavior acceptable then I was accepted. It was a false sense of belonging.

Meanwhile, as the enemy was ensnaring my life, my mom would pray Psalm 91 over me. She would fill my name in the spots where the psalmist would refer to self or I. She said she once told the Lord that she couldn't say those things about me because I wasn't living the way the psalm went, but He instructed her that I did love Him and to say those things. Below I have included some portions of Psalm 91.

He who dwells in the secret place of the Most High Shall abide under the shadow of the Almighty. I will say of the LORD, "He is my refuge and my fortress; My God, in Him I will trust." You shall not be afraid of the terror by night, Nor of the arrow that flies by day, Because you have made the LORD, who is my refuge, Even the Most High, your dwelling place, No evil shall befall you, Nor shall any plague come near your dwelling; For He shall give His angels charge over you, To keep you in all your ways. Because he has set his love upon Me, therefore I will deliver him; I will set him on high, because he has known My name. He shall call upon Me, and I will answer him; I will be with him in trouble; I will deliver him and honor him. With long life I will satisfy

him, And show him My salvation.
(Psalm 91:1–5, 9-11, 14–16 NKJV)

She prayed that over me and kept believing God was at work. No matter how difficult the situation grew, she pressed on. Because you see, she learned to walk by faith and not go by how bad the situation seemed (2 Corinthians 5:7). She learned that the word of God doesn't return void, but He sees to it that the promises come about (Isaiah 55:11). If you have a spouse, child, or family member you are believing will come home to the family of God, I highly recommend praying that over him or her. It's not a magic formula. However, it is an incredibly powerful passage of scripture.

I continued through college while drinking and still maintaining good grades. In addition, it was a Christian university, and because I was so "churched" I could easily outshine my peers in knowledge of certain biblical topics. I was disengaged with life, and I pretty much mocked

Christianity. I felt like God wasn't who He said He was and Christians were simply following a pipe dream. I even got into an argument in class with one of my professors because I was adamant people follow God for fear of consequences, while he adamantly stated the complete opposite, that indeed people follow Christ for the sake of love. I didn't buy it. I graduated with a BA in psychology and continued to work to support myself. I made a lot of poor choices during that time. I was in my early twenties when I had very little contact with my parents and family. I continued to become more calloused. I was angry at Christians because I felt they were self-righteous. I was living life with this giant hole in my heart and trying to fill it with empty promises. There is nothing outside of Jesus that will fill that. Nothing. I self-medicated by drinking almost every day because I didn't know how to manage my life. I was foolishly trying to avoid the pain by focusing on me. I was incredibly self-absorbed. That's what pain will do to us. It causes our tragedies to become our trophies.

> **That's what pain will do to us. It causes our tragedies to become our trophies.**

This is precisely why I'm so thankful it says so beautifully and powerfully in Isaiah just how much Jesus loves us:

But the fact is, it was our pains he carried—our disfigurements, all the things wrong with us. We thought he brought it on himself, that God was punishing him for his own failures. But it was our sins that did that to him, that ripped and tore and crushed him—our sins! He took the punishment, and that made us whole. Through his bruises we get healed. We're all like sheep who've wandered off and gotten lost. We've all done our own thing, gone our own way. And GOD has piled all our sins, everything we've done wrong, on him, on him. (Isaiah 53:4–6 MSG)

I was in a terrible car accident that should have seriously injured or killed me, and I walked away. One would think that would be a wakeup call, but it wasn't. I told my parents Jesus had rescued me and I had changed. It was a wonderful glimpse of the daughter they once knew. And were eager to see the years of poor choices finally end. However, shortly after I went back to my same old lifestyle. I looked for His hand of provision to still give me what I wanted and needed. Sadly, I wouldn't look into His eyes. Because I was afraid. I didn't want to look up. I didn't want to see the love in His eyes that burn like fire. I settled for a handout instead of His heart.

I settled for a handout instead of His heart.

It got to the point where I knew I was going to lose my job from the drinking, and it wasn't going to be much longer that I could carry on. I wasn't eating again. I was so out of control and felt captive. I was done, and I just wanted to escape. During this pain, I distinctly remember the feeling of not wanting to be alone. I remember looking at women who would be sitting at the bar in their fifties and sixties groveling for attention and trying to recapture their youth. And I realized I was making choice after choice that was propelling me right down that road as well. I knew I couldn't outrun time and eventually I would be one of them.

Even in the moments of self-medicating and making incredibly poor choices, I would have moments of knowing I needed to somehow find my way back home. My life was chaotic, and I was frantically grasping for control. I had tried church, and I had tried living life my own way, and if I were completely honest with myself, I knew I wanted God. I would think of those moments as a kid when God was real in the services and healing people and setting them free. I knew there was safety in following Him. But then temptation would overshadow those memories, and my resolve was gone. I remember I was encouraged to take the step to live a life of freedom—that God wasn't going to just rescue me, that I was going to have to choose to partner with Him. Many people want the easy way, and that seldom happens. I was going to have to move from the small town I was in because I wasn't strong enough to say no to the people I was hanging around with. I didn't have accountability. I knew I was going to have to move and quit my job. This is just me, but I am going to share with you what I believe to be one of the key factors for me in turning my heart back to God and deciding to take the first step.

There has been an incredible movement about the love of God for the past fifteen years. While it has set many free and brought about tremendous healing, I believe another piece is also true. God is love (1 John 4:8). He is also to be feared. It says in Proverbs 9:10 (GW), "The fear of the Lord is the beginning of wisdom." If we take away the wisdom, then we're left with a frenzy. And that's just not fun for anyone.

It was the fear of knowing I was going to be *out of relationship* with people I cared about deeply. Yes, my family loved me, but they also set good boundaries. They didn't care to indulge me or pity me in my poor choices. I cannot speak enough about this. They didn't enable me to think it was no big deal. It wasn't a big deal to me because I wasn't living the reality they were in because I was self-medicating by drinking. However, it was a big deal to them. It broke their hearts. Let me very clear in this. They were not rude, nor were they unkind. They weren't any of that. They simply chose not to participate with me in my world.

So how does this relate to fearing the Lord? Well, I believe one aspect of it is fearing the things that break His heart. Broken families and fractured relationships are costly, and they mean the world to Him, so much that He sent His Son to a world that wasn't in relationship with Him. John 3:16 (KJV) says, "For God so loved the world that He gave His only begotten Son." For God so loved you. He had you in mind when He sent Jesus to die for you. That's incredible love, and that's the love of your Father. He wants to know you. He wants to be in relationship with you. Why? Because He likes you. He really, really, really likes and loves you.

Let me ask you this: "What's not to love about you?" Let me say there wasn't one thing that came to His mind about you that stopped Him from sending His Son to die for you. *Not one thing about you could stop His love.* If you are protesting in your mind thinking how sinful you are, thinking about a bunch of poor choices you've made, that you aren't worthy, or that it's too late for you, read what I'm about to say slowly and let it sink in. *He said while you were yet sinning He died for you (Romans 5:8). Yes, that's right. While you were still making one poor choice after another, He wanted you to know His incredible love that would set you free.* With you in mind, He had every reason to send Jesus to be beaten, bloodied, die and resurrected so you could know His endless love.

Just as He chose us in Him before the foundation of the world, that we should be holy and without blame before Him in love. (Ephesians 1:4 NKJV).

Beloved, He doesn't look at you with disapproval and disappointment! Oh how deep and wide is His love for you (see Ephesians 3:18). When you are in Christ, all He sees is love. He is not looking at you with the glare of a disappointed Father. You delight Him. He loves you. *You are not in trouble.* You are welcomed into His everlasting love.

With you in mind, He had every reason to send Jesus to be beaten and bloodied, to die, and be resurrected so you could know His endless love.

Through many prayers and some honest conversations, I swallowed my pride and in 2007 I moved in with my parents. Honestly, I don't even know how I had any pride, but hey, when you are deceived, you don't think straight. They graciously opened their home and hearts to their prodigal daughter. God has a funny way of working things out, doesn't He? He sent me back to the very place I thought I was running from. Please read that last sentence one more time. Sometimes we won't go back physically, but we will go back. If the process was tweaked or short circuited, then He's going to lead you through it. I'm not talking about reliving hellish situations. Not at all. I'm talking about helping you find truth, value, your voice, your identity, and your purpose that were lost. He wastes nothing. "We know that all things work together for the good of those who love God" (Romans 8:28 GW).

CHAPTER 6

HOME SWEET HOME

Because I can be described as someone who just says it how it is (ask me later how that's been working for me), that's pretty much what took place when I went home to live with my parents. I wanted this "religion" thing to work. I sincerely did. But I didn't want to walk down a road that wasn't worth walking down. You might be wondering if I'm incredibly dull in thinking to say that considering I had already walked down many roads not worth walking. However, the reality was I needed God desperately. I didn't know how He was going to sort through the mess in my soul, and I didn't want my heart broken if

He didn't come through. So I told God I wanted our relationship to be nothing like it was when I was growing up. And you know what? It hasn't been. I started to go back to church. That was basic and foundational.

Going back to church was like home sweet home! It's the place where the wayward and the wearied find rest. A place where the forgotten and the abandoned are known by name. A place where people can talk about life, issues, and problems. Yet when the hours have gone by, people find connection and belonging. It's a place where stories of redemption are told—a place where friendships are forged. The church is a place where you see kindness extended and strangers smitten by their shared passions. It's a place where enthusiasm is rekindled, where hopelessness has left its empty promises. It's a place where people dare to show up and to embrace brokenness without it becoming an identity worn shamefully. It's where the prodigal and the preacher find a place to call home. It's like home sweet home because Jesus can be found there. It wasn't just a social club.

I fell in love with the church and realized how incredibly wonderful the church family is! With all her uniqueness and differences, I found the church. I was home, and I didn't want to ever go back to anything else. It was then that God began to in His great mercy unwrap the layers and layers and layers of pain on my life. Something that spared me much heartache and confusion was the role mature Christian women played in my growing process, and they were incredible examples to me. I saw their commitment to God and their unwavering faith in Him despite hard and difficult circumstances. I watched mature believers continue to run their race for years and never give up. They didn't allow the journey to overshadow their faith in God. I marveled at this. I am so incredibly thankful to God for these saints! One particular passage of scripture can describe them:

They didn't allow the journey to overshadow their faith in God.

But be careful that by using your freedom you don't somehow make a believer who is weak in faith fall into sin. For example, suppose someone with a weak conscience sees you, who have this knowledge, eating in the temple of a false god. Won't you be encouraging that person to eat food offered to a false god? In that case, your knowledge is ruining a believer whose faith is weak, a believer for whom Christ died. When you sin against other believers in this way and harm their weak consciences, you are sinning against Christ. Therefore, if eating food offered to false gods causes other believers to lose their faith, I will never eat that kind of food so that I won't make other believers

lose their faith. (2 Corinthians 8:9–
13 GW)

I get that Paul is talking about food offered to
idols, but do you get the overall reason why he
is willing to not eat the food? Because he valued
family and relationship more than his liberty.
Family was his priority. I was one of those young
ones. I had a weak conscious, and the last thing in
the world I needed to see was those women who
I looked up to walking around with wine glasses
in their hands to help them relax or unwind.
It was wanting to unwind that led me down a
path of "needing" to drink daily. I never thought
it would become that. Consequently, I needed
victory. I needed hope. I was a slave to sin, and I
was begging someone to help me find my way out
of it. Yes, it's ultimately Jesus who does, but He
uses the community and family around us too.
Unfortunately, I saw other Christians drinking
and allowed that to be my standard and not
the women in my life who weren't. And what
God had to show my stubborn heart was either

I wanted Him or I didn't. It was foolish of me to want freedom from something to then think I could just have a glass here and there. And it took a very long and painful road for me to discover that freedom cost His son's life. He wasn't looking for me to play games with His heart. In His great mercy, it's been years since I've had a sip.

This isn't to make anyone feel guilty. This isn't to bring shame. Not at all. This is to simply share some of my story. There is a world that is lost in pain, rejection, and abandonment, and Satan has used every vice possible to destroy them. They are crying out for something real—for the church to show them victory and hope. And while I may not be drinking, I have to live this out too. Trust me. I have to choose daily and in so many ways how I will live my life for His glory. I feel like my brother and sister were born nice. They enjoy people. They are kind. They are funny and sensitive. They don't get too bothered by things. They forgive easily. People flock to them. They just enjoy life. My personality tends to lean the other way. I must work really hard at each of those things. I tend to be too intense, while they are even-keeled. I have so much still to learn.

It's not about never sinning or having the perfect lifestyle but rather choosing Him over and over. And over. It makes my heart skip a beat and smile even as I write that. Do you know what it does to His heart when you choose Him? It becomes a relationship. To this day, choosing Him has been by far the most rewarding part of my spiritual journey. It makes me so happy knowing the joy it brings to His heart when we choose Him. Being in relationship with Him is incredibly fun!

CHAPTER 7

LESSONS LEARNED ALONG
THE JOURNEY

I talked to people who had been running the
race a lot longer than myself and asked them
about good books to read. It was like being in
love for the first time. I wanted to know as much
as I could about God. I wanted to hear and read
different perspectives and soak in as much as I
could. In that, I am very selective on what I read
or listen to. In the age of Google, I find there is
too much available for young Christ followers. I
also listened to hundreds of sermons and podcasts
and included fasting and praying as part of my

spiritual disciplines. I also learned the power of speaking the word of God out loud. Jesus is our model, and when He was tempted in the wilderness, He didn't just think His way out of the situation. He spoke the word out loud (see Matthew 4:10).

I learned that despite my feelings, the Bible is a stronger reality. I also learned that not all emotions or thoughts are ours, that the enemy plants seeds in our minds and emotions. For years, I lived under the constant sway of whatever came at me. This included fear, hopelessness, poor relationship choices, etc. For example, if I had feelings for someone who wasn't a healthy potential partner, I would simply think I must have changed my mind about that person. The temptation was subtle, and I failed to recognize it was the enemy wanting me to make another bad decision. Instead, I should have chosen to cast down those false imaginations and resisted the devil (see 2 Corinthians 10:5, James 4:7).

One particular learning lesson I had was when I was having anxiety and fear—you know, the kind that seems to replay the absolute worst-case scenario over and over in your mind. Well, being the outspoken and somewhat intense person that I can be, I told Him that He was supposed to keep me in perfect peace, to which He calmly replied in my heart, "I said if. I will keep you in perfect peace *if* your mind is stayed on Me." See Isaiah 26:3. Suddenly, it became very clear. He promises to do a lot—more than you or I can ever imagine or know.

However, sometimes there is a part we get to play, and it's called being in relationship. He doesn't force or coerce us, nor does He want to carry around babies. We are called to mature. What parent wants their child to never mature? He enjoys the process with us and the stages. But His design isn't for us to stay stuck in any of those stages. He wants to share the process with us. When we progress from stage to stage, it gives Him such joy and delight. Just like parents who practically throw their backs out running for their camera when they see their baby taking their first steps, He, too, delights in our process and progress!

As I mentioned, I had struggled with an eating disorder since I was in the eighth grade. While medical professionals will tell you that it's a lifetime diagnosis, my Bible says Jesus is my healer. "He sent His Word and healed them and delivered them from their destructions" (Psalm 107:20 KJV). I had always used not eating as a way of escape—the desire for control and comfort. One day, I remember I was in my dining room, and I was playing my keyboard worshiping Jesus. I was enjoying the time together when I felt Him speak to my heart that I had made a covenant with a false comforter. I was finding comfort in the control. He went on to remind me in scripture it says the Holy Spirit is our comforter (John 14:26). He alone is to have that role. Period. I said a very simple prayer of repentance and out loud broke my agreement with a false comfort in Jesus' name. I was healed in that moment.

He went on to remind me in scripture
it says the Holy Spirit is our comforter.
He alone is to have that role.

That was years ago, and the desire to partner with that has come back once for less than a twenty-four-hour period. I didn't give in and went on to eat as usual. A lifetime struggle was healed in that moment when I finally understood the spiritual implications of what my choices were doing. He is a faithful and delivering God! Nothing is too hard for Him! If He can do it for me, He can do it for you! What are you finding false comfort in, my friend? Maybe it's food, maybe it's spending, maybe it's your job, maybe it's prescription drug abuse. Whatever it is, ask Him. Ask Him to heal you just like He did for me. Break the agreement with a false comfort, ask for Him to forgive you, and thank the Holy Spirit for His help and that He is your new comfort. Nothing is too hard for His love! "Ah, Lord GOD … There is nothing too hard for You" (Jeremiah 32:17 NKJV).

CHAPTER 8

KINDNESS IS UNFORGETTABLE

> What man of you, having a hundred sheep, if he loses one of them, does not leave the ninety-nine in the wilderness, and go after the one which is lost until he finds it? And when he has found it, he lays it on his shoulders, rejoicing. (Luke 15:4–5 NKJV)

My brother often teases me about literally having stories about nothing. He says I can make something very simple a story. I can walk to the post office and come back with two normal things that don't mean anything to anyone else, except I will find a way to make a story out of them. It makes me smile even thinking about it now. Little did he realize he was only encouraging me to write and someday publish a book.

Close to ten years ago, I decided it would be really fun to throw a party. I figured I knew plenty of people who weren't that busy who surely would want to come join this barrel of fun. I decided to ask someone to host it with me, and she graciously obliged. Truthfully, she knew a lot more people than I did and had a lot more friends. I was so excited as I drew up the guest list and began to plan. There wasn't Pinterest then, so it took more time and effort. E-vites were fairly new, so I thought I was being rather "cutting edge" in using it to send out the cute party invitations.

It wasn't a special occasion or anything like that. I just wanted to gather people. I made up the invitation list of I think fifteen to twenty invites. I hit the send button and went to work on getting the party planned. I don't recall exactly how much time went by but I would guess around a week or longer, and I failed to get much of a response. My heart sank. I thought it was such a good idea. Ever have a good idea? Ever have one not turn out like you thought? Well, this was that moment for me right there. I'm literally throwing a party and no one can come, or worse yet I thought, *Does no one* want *to come? I'm not a high school kid trying to fit in. I am a grown adult. A grown adult trying to throw a party that is soon becoming not much of anything.*

Realizing at this point that it probably was only going to be me and my co-hostess attending, I thought I might want to think about something else. So, I had another good idea. There is a story in the Bible about a man who threw a party (Luke 14:15–24), and people did not come, so he invited the poor. That got my wheels spinning. So, I decided to make flyers about the party. They were nothing fancy. I made them and printed them out. I had no friend to grab on this particular day, so I went solo.

I drove down to where a government food truck would come and drop off food. I found many people standing in line waiting. I walked up to people and introduced myself. I then passed out the flyers and invited them to the party. I told them it was free and they could come enjoy games and food. I stayed for the whole event and chatted with the people who were there.

The food line was over, and I decided to go pray. I was exhausted. I was wondering if anyone would come to the party. Yes, my heart hurt. I felt rejected. I felt a lot of emotions. I remember praying for I think close to two hours when I felt the Lord speak to my heart that He celebrates the one. It was an answer from heaven that invaded my world. You may be thinking, *Whoa there, sister, a little dramatic.* Wait. The story isn't over. Remember? I like to tell stories, and I like to build up to the best part.

Party day arrived, and I carried on like a party was happening. Seriously, I had no idea if anyone would come. My fellow hostess and I brought food and got some music going (I think to calm our nerves more than anything and fill the silence). The table was set with food, and games were ready. We were there. I don't know how long this "party" was going—perhaps fifteen minutes or so—when in walked one family. *One*. I was so excited I can't tell you! He celebrates the one! We brought them in, and we ate together and their children played. We talked, and I got to know them. The night continued as we chatted about wherever the conversation led us to … and you know what, my friend? They were the *one*. One beautiful family came to my party. One.

You see, if I hadn't spent time with Him, pouring out before Him on what was going on I can't say I would've had hope. But because He told me He celebrates the one, then I did too. That one family grew to having family nights once a month. By the end of around five months of having family nights, it grew to 150 people attending. Why? Because He celebrates the one.

I don't know what you are facing right now. Maybe you are in a place where you had a good idea and you thought it was supposed to work out a certain way, and it didn't. Maybe you are wondering if you are throwing another party to be the only one attending. It may not look like what you thought it was supposed to look like, but He has a plan. He knows. Maybe it's your life not turning out as you had hoped. Or a failed marriage. The loss of a job. But maybe for now, it's being intentionally kind to the one He places in front of us. Each day. Every day.

Ironically, the story doesn't stop there. Last year I was told about a woman who knows me and talks about me, and I could not figure out how she did. I asked the person how this lady knows me, and it was from the food drive. I had helped carry food to her car one time, and she hadn't forgotten. Kindness is unforgettable. I know there has been a lot of tension in America during and even since the 2016 presidential campaign process, and this isn't meant to turn political. Unfortunately, I have seen many people continue to sacrifice relationships on the altar of rightness. I have to wonder if it is ever really worth it.

What I can say is there's nothing worse than a fighting mom and dad in a house. When mom and dad are fighting, the whole house knows it, and no one wants to be home. The family becomes affected by the atmosphere. Kids go and hide in their rooms or turn their earbuds on. They don't want to hear it. In the same fashion, the church family did a lot of fighting, and the world didn't want to hear it. They still don't.

We forgot we are accepted in the Beloved and we try to force others to accept our way of thinking. We aren't meant to compromise. Not at all. We were just never meant to get into a fight. The church family looks a little crueler than it did a year ago, and it breaks my heart because I love our family, and I like our family—as does God. If you want to be remembered and known for something, let your kindness be unforgettable.

If you want to be remembered and known for something, let your kindness be unforgettable.

CHAPTER 9

EXPECTATIONS:
RELATIONSHIP KILLERS

Growing up I never realized the sacrifices my parents had made—the times the pressure was overwhelming and they forged ahead. My dad grew up with a "man's man" dad. There wasn't a lot of affection, and consequently it's not been a strong point for my dad either. But what I can say is I saw a man who knows how to cast out demons, a man who sticks to the word of God and doesn't waver, a man who works hard and doesn't quit, a man who provides for his family even when he's working three jobs to do so, a man who didn't give up on his daughter when she was a disgrace to the family, a man who kept pointing me to Jesus no matter what, a man who didn't quit the ministry when he could've many times over.

I saw a man who showed up to our games when he was tired from working. I saw a man who kept pursuing God even when church attendance fluctuated. My dad has a backbone of iron, and I thank God for what he has modeled for my life. Dad, well done. You did it. You are doing it. I'm so proud of you.

My mom is as sweet as can be. To know her is truly to love her. I've watched as her identity in Christ has become her truth, and the impact of that knowledge has empowered the people around her. She is passionate about helping others know their value. One of the *most* incredible inheritances my mom has given me is watching her have her devotions every morning. I've learned that if I want to be a woman who succeeds, I have to put God first.

I watched as the Bible became her weapon of choice in life. She would speak the word over situations, problems, and brokenness. And I watched as she prayed and answers would come. She never swerved. She has run the race that was set before her. She didn't stop, she didn't give up, she didn't break down, and she kept going day after day and year after year. Mom, well done. You've maintained your beauty, your boldness, your truth through the journey. I'm so proud of you. I love you.

Over the years, I have had the immense pleasure of speaking with parents who have raised their kids in Christian homes. I have shared tears with some and even wondered why God in His mercy allowed me to find my way home and not their children. I have seen the most beautiful Christians grapple with why their kids aren't attending church or serving God. Those have been some painful moments for me personally. I have to wonder why am I any different than other children raised in church. Why haven't others decided to go back to church? And to be honest, I don't have an answer. I wish I did. Maybe that's why I'm writing this book—because we're family and because we belong together and my heart is breaking. I want them to come home.

Dear one, if you have children or a child who is not serving Jesus, do not give up! No matter how dark their lives look and how many poor choices they are making, do not give up. In this book, I gave you a very short, condensed version of what exactly transpired, but I can assure you I broke my parents hearts a thousand times for *years*, never realizing their own pain and the battles they were in, not to mention the countless sacrifices they were making.

I don't care if you think you could have done better parenting. I don't care if it's what you knew at the time. I beg you to receive the mercy of God and forgive yourself. Your child's personal choices are not your fault. Let that sink in. Just because your child has experienced a lot of pain or a lot of heartache doesn't mean you were a bad parent. I bless you now in Jesus' name to receive His great grace. Especially in Christian circles or if you are in ministry, there is no shame in where your children are at spiritually. If your children are not serving Jesus, do not fear and do not be ashamed. The Lord loves them dearly. He loves them. He so dearly loves them. Do not give up! He hasn't given up on them.

And for you, dear one, if you are a child who is still struggling with your relationship with your parents (whether or not they were in ministry), let your parents go. Forgive and release them. I am not saying you will have a perfect relationship with them, and there may be some legitimate boundaries that need to be in place. But I beg you to quit holding them hostage in your soul. You may be thinking yes, but ... but what? I remember my beloved mentor, Mama C, saying to me that I must lose the perfectionism I have. Expectations are relationship killers. It set me free. It can set you free too. No parent is perfect.

No parent may recognize or own their stuff entirely … but you don't control them. You can only control you with the help of the Holy Spirit. So let go of the perfectionistic expectations, and watch what God does. This is a continued process. It doesn't happen once, and you are done. I mistakenly thought that. Nope, it's a continual process of forgiving and loving. They get to do this with you as well, because you aren't perfect either.

Expectations are relationship killers.

If you have read this book and don't have parents who know Jesus or maybe want someone to fill that place in your life, then ask. I'm not talking about replacing your parents, but rather having spiritual parents in your life. Don't be afraid to reach out and talk to your pastor or small group leader on who a good recommendation could be in your church. I prayed and asked the Lord to send me a mentor when I lived far away from my own parents. He did. Don't get mixed up on the age either. Sometimes a spiritual "parent" may be younger than you if he or she has a mature walk with God.

> **More than ever the church must be**
> **ready for the great journey home.**
> **It's coming. It's happening.**

If you are a mature Christian, I ask that you start mentoring young ones. Be available. Now is not the time to leave home. We need you. You have a place in the family! You are not unwanted. We need your example, your encouragement, your wisdom! You have so much to bless the younger generations with! We need you to be present. Now isn't the time to check out and begin traveling and be in and out of our lives. You have so much to impart. Consider being family mentors with your spouse. Bless a family once a month, and offer to take them out to dinner, to encourage them periodically with scripture. Give them date night and watch their kids if they have little ones. Come alongside the family and offer support.

If you don't have the time to commit to that, be a mentor to a young woman, and if you are a guy, be a mentor to a young man. Take the time. The journey home isn't always easy. Sometimes when you get there, you are unprepared for it. You need help in your spiritual progress. You may need help with your marriage or finances. It's not time to be alone. More than ever the church must be ready for the great journey home. It's coming. It's happening.

CHAPTER 10

ꙮ

FINDING YOUR WAY HOME

Did I ever get all my questions answered from chapter 1? No, beloved, I didn't, and they don't matter to me as much. He is God; I am not. That's why it's called faith. It's trusting His goodness for my life despite feelings and circumstances that try to catapult my life into agnosticism. I have found that everything around us changes. Everything. And yet, His compassion fails not (Lamentations 3:22). Like the disciples, I have found myself saying I have nowhere else to go. He has the words of life (John 6:68). I can say His faithfulness and nature far surpassed my disappointments. He is lovely, generous, kind, and beautiful. My heart is full just thinking about His goodness. The years of heartache were redeemed through His tender love.

When your heart hurt, so did His.

I ask, whether you are a Christ follower or not, "What do you need Him to be for you today, dear reader?" You might be still struggling with something or someone and think you cannot ask Him for anything. Or maybe you're thinking He hasn't been there for you like you thought He would. Or why something was allowed to happen if He is good. Or maybe it's the church family you have a problem with and not God.

As much as we all have questions or things we don't understand, this I can say: *when your heart hurt, so did His.* How could it not? You are His child. He is a Father who loves you and cares so much about you. Have you ever seen a grandparent talk about his or her grandkids? Or a new mom? Moms will flip through their smartphones with blinding accuracy as they look for the most recent picture of their little ones. The same goes for your father God. It says in Isaiah 49:15 (MSG): "But even if mothers forget, I'd never forget you." It goes on to say in verse 16 that you are inscribed on His hands. He holds up His hand and looks at you—in absolute awe of you. You are never far from His loving gaze.

I pray in this moment you understand the love He has for you. Forgive Him. Forgive yourself, and forgive the church if that's where the wounding came from. No one can ever make up for the pain. Only Jesus can heal that. Take the journey home. Beloved, it's worth every step you take to get there. Your story is not over. No sin is too great. No disappointment is too big. He has a great plan for your life. And remember to allow yourself mistakes. It's not about our perfection. It's about not quitting. Nothing on earth compares to being home and being a part of the family. He is such a wonderful Father!

Take the journey home. Beloved, it's worth every step you take to get there.

In closing, thank you for taking the time for reading this book and sharing the journey home with me. I am forever grateful. Maybe you are home and you haven't found your place. I pray you do. I pray you understand the immense pleasure you bring to your Father and to the family of God. You have purpose. You have value. You belong, more than you could ever imagine. I pray you understand the immense joy of being a part of the family and the love of the Father. You don't know what you're missing. There's nothing like being home.

> Prayer:
> Father, I am in need of You, and I'm ready to come home.
> I believe Jesus died for my sins, and I want to be your child.
> I have spent so much time away from You and Your family.

I ask that You forgive me for walking away and for allowing hurt to control my life.

I confess my pride before You and ask that you forgive me of all my sins.

I ask now that You would be number one in every area of my life, even in the places that You haven't been.

Thank You for accepting me. Help me to find a family and a place to call home.

I look forward to the journey with You by my side.

I love You.

In Jesus' Name,
Amen

The Words

Welcome home! Now you are home and a part of the family. I've included a short list of confessions to say out loud and partner your faith with.

- God is not mad or disappointed with me (Zephaniah 3:17).

- God accepts me (Ephesians 1:6).

- My past doesn't dictate my future (Philippians 3:13).

- I am not a victim (2 Timothy 1:7).

- I have God's peace even in the storms of life (Isaiah 54:10).

- I have value and worth (Luke 12:7).

- God is on my side (Romans 8:31).

- I am submitted to God and His ways (James 4:7).

- The Holy Spirit is my comforter (John 14:16, John 14:26).

- God is working out situations in my life for my good (Romans 8:28).

- My life isn't based on what people say about me (Galatians 1:10).

- I am the righteousness of God (2 Corinthians 5:21).

- God is my shield and defense (Psalm 59:9, 17, 94:22).

- I am not always going to be this way. Every day I'm changing into His image (2 Corinthians 3:18).

- I am learning to love difficult people (Romans 5:5).

- I am loving, joyful, peaceful, patient, good, kind, faithful, gentle, and self-controlled (Galatians 5:22–23).

- I have vision for my life (Proverbs 29:18).

- I don't react to life situations out of past wounds (2 Corinthians 5:17).

- People are not my problem (Ephesians 6:12).

- God is a priority in my life (Matthew 6:33).

- I am not afraid to try new things (Isaiah 41:10).

- My best days are ahead of me (1 Corinthians 2:9, Ephesians 2:10).

- I am not easily offended (Matthew 18:21–22).

- I am confident in His good plan for my life (Jeremiah 29:11).

- I think like Jesus (1 Corinthians 2:16).

- The family of God is a priority in my life (Galatians 6:10, Hebrews 10:25).

Printed in the United States
By Bookmasters